The Devil Drives A Black Volga

A Collection of ~~Poems~~
and Short Stories

J Elmore

J. ELMORE

For more information or to book an event, contact : jelmorebooks@gmail.com
http://www.jelmorebooks.com

Cover design by John thomas Oaks

ISBN - Paperback: 9798850919481

First Edition: August 2023

Table of Contents

J. Elmore

Lo, How the Nightingale Spreadeth His Wings

Lo, how the nightingale spreadeth his wings,

To mimic the notes that a goldfinch wouldst sing.

He riseth above through the blackness of night,

Guided by only the soft lunar light.

He cascadeth down from his realm in the sky,

And affixeth himself where my Adelaide lies.

Where Adelaide lies, where her spirit did

cease,

Seen only by stars, seen only by trees.

The bird singeth sorrow, a pilgrim of air;

As he entagl'th his claws in sweet Adelaide's hair.

In singing, he mourneth, to cry for my love,

My honor'd of queens, my virtue of doves.

Forever unknown, forever unseen:

Untold by the stars, untold by the trees.

Wisteria

Immortality is immunity,

To sickness and to Death;

Sleeping lazily,

Dreaming hazily,

Safe nonetheless.

But is there any valor

In a mere protection spell?

Never dying,

Never fighting,

Always safe and well?

Instead, look to Wisteria,

Which dies, as humans do;

But when tangled, strangled,

Maimed and mangled,

It grows its vines anew.

Ode to the Dragon King

In mountain air where wingéd creatures fly,
Near Inverness, a rocky moor didst stand.
There in a cave, a noble dragon lies;
Till dusk he waits to lark about the land.

His home he leaves beneath the rising
moon,
For gathering his lavender and thyme.
But as the sun appears above the dunes,
He sleepily sneaks to his tranquil clime.

For day is when the fearsome creatures
prowl,

Only bearing two legs for their stride.

To flee the grasp of such a creature foul,

Inside his cave the dragon safely hides.

Concealed and shrouded in his cloak of
stone,

The peaceful dragon king reigns all alone.

S o n h a d o r a

On a hill near the coast were four beautiful trees. Often would a young traveler find them on her journey to the sea and resolve to rest in their shade.

She came running from the mountains that July. She looked not unlike the others, with eyes of the brightest sort and hair dancing merrily in dark coils. I saw her nearly fall to the ground in exhaustion when she reached the top of the hill.

"Come, *sonhadora*[1], rest," a voice called

---

[1] Portuguese word meaning, "dreamer."

behind her. She turned, but no one was found save the four trees. "Look not to the sea, but to us," it spoke, "for we have all the answers you seek."

She searched around her again. "Who are you?"

"I am Pequizeiro," said the first tree. "My branches are tangled from reaching deep within the souls of troubled humans. The fruit I produce is soft and sweet but full of dangerous spikes on the inside. Rest in my shade, and I will reveal to you all the secrets of your very spirit."

"I am Jequitibá," said the second tree. "I am very old and very strong. I have lived through many wars, rulers, and governments. Rest in my shade, and I will tell you all of the secrets of the world- sciences, history, and mathematics; all that has existed since the beginning of time."

"I am Ipe-Rosa," said the third tree. "Strangers from all over the world are enticed by my beauty, and they share secrets as they sit beneath my branches. I hear whispers of all things—even some, perhaps, regarding you. Rest in my shade, and I will tell you all of the forbidden knowledge of the hearts of humankind."

"I am Araucária," said the last tree. "I am extremely tall, and I can see all of what happens in the world and all that is soon to come. Rest in my shade, and I will tell you the future."

When the trees had finished speaking, the young sonhadora turned and heard my cries rising softly on the breeze. "Who are you?" she asked.

"I am the sea," said I. "My shores have been touched by the shade of all four trees. I know the darkest secrets within my soul. I know what the mighty Pacific whispers when she speaks of me to her sailors. I am familiar with all worldly wisdom, and I have seen the future. Do not rest under these trees, for I have seen it all, and I can only weep bitterly. Go home, my dear sonhadora, live in peace."

To Me, They Spoke of Love

There were rumors of our leaders,

That their reign would never cease;

But I did not hear their idle talk-

To me, they spoke of peace.

There were beggars on the corners,

With a drink in hand to cope;

But I did not hear their drunken cries-

To me, they spoke of hope.

There was nothing in the cupboards,

We'd begun to lose our strength;

But they did not let me grumble much-

To me, they spoke of faith.

In the books, they'll speak of warfare,

Blazing fires from above;

But the books will not remember this:

To me, they spoke of love.

The Queen of Bodmin Moor

Tread about the Bodmin Moor,
Until the moorland's Queen you find;
Rest beside her cottage door,
And in that shelter safely hide.

For when comes morn, so comes the Queen,
Beclothed in golden rays of sun;
She dances 'cross the meadows green,
And follows where the rivers run.

When she finds you, ask to stay,
And cast away your sword and shield;

For she may choose to grant your name
To century-plants throughout the field.

Rest, *marchogion*[2], live in peace,
And leave your sword with Bodmin's Queen.

---

[2] Welsh soldier.

The Fall of Assur

In the days of Urartu, in Tushpa
The land was taken and given to Assur.
And the queen they called Susaratu
along with all people, was taken and given
to Assur.

All people were made subjects of Assur:
to sow the ground in Assur, and build things
in Assur forever.
Susaratu was kept hidden while her people
worked and her city burned.
And she was held over their heads for forty
days,
for forty days Assur said, "She will be

released to you;

she will work among you!

but if you step outside the walls of Assur, if

you take our food and gold for your own;

if you rise against the King of Assur;

her death will stain your conscience."

At the end of the forty days,

Susaratu was brought before her people,

and a sword was brought over her head.

But before the blade came down, she

cursed the city, saying:

"Assur has dishonored its promise to my
people

and my blood will be on its hands.

It will cry out in hunger and thirst,

but its desperation will never be consoled.

It will wash its hands to be cleansed of my
blood;

but like a sheep before wild dogs, it is

marked for destruction.

Even when its own stench overcomes it and
it turns its face away to vomit,
even then it will find no relief."

When she finished saying these things, they
killed her in the presence of her people,
and her body burned.

On the forty-first day since the capture of
Susaratu,
the King of Assur held a feast.
Every nobleman, every commander, and
many landowners were in attendance.

The finest wine was brought from Urartu
and dancers and musicians from Tushpa
were made to perform in mockery of their
queen. The palace gates were shut,
and every door was barricaded so that no
performers could escape.
After the first song,
the King spoke to all the people, saying,

"Hail to the Queen of Urartu,
whose blood we have spilled with our own
hands!"
He lifted a glass of wine, and every
partygoer followed
(as was the custom).

But when the wine touched their lips, it
became blood,
and every Assyrian who drank fell to the
ground.
They crawled toward the locked doors,
and wailed at the gates,
but the Urartian musicians who were not
permitted to drink seized weapons from the
fallen soldiers
and speared everyone to death.

The stench of blood from the palace grew
so strong that everyone in Assur could smell
it. People in all parts of the city were so
overcome by the smell

that they began to vomit.
And the Urartian musicians who were still
within the palace made piles of the dead
Assyrians,
and the piles grew so high that they could
be used to scale the gates.
And every Urartian escaped the palace
alive.

They spread the news that the King and all
his commanders were dead,
and every Urartian in Assur took for
themselves a spear
and put every Assyrian man, woman, and
child to death.
All of the King's gold was taken,
and the palace was burned.

And the Urartians traveled across Assyria,
taking with them the Scythians,
and burned every Assyrian city to the
ground.

They returned to Urartu,

taking with them the ashes of Susaratu,

and they made the musician Adilshevas

their king.

And the glory of Tushpa was restored.

Надежда

*Письмо   солдата   к   его
возлюбленной,   около
1941- ого   года,
после   первой   битвы
под   Киевом.*

Мне кажется, сегодня,

В небе света нет.

К несчастью, моя девочка,

К нам не придет рассвет.

Пожалуйста, моя сладкая,

Не уходи, когда

Уходят вещи дорогие,

И угасает надежда вся.

Помни, если грустно,

Главное, что я понял:

Береги себя, прости себя,

И подумай о том, что сказал:

Если есть огонь,

       пусть горит.

Если есть любовь,

       не дай умереть.

У кого есть вера?

       не забывай;

И кто знает Бога?

       Его и умоляй.

N a d e z h d a

Pismo soldata k evo
vozlyublennoy,
okolo 1941-ogo
goda, posle pervoy
bitvy pod Kievom.

Mne kazhetsya, sevodnya,

V nebe sveta net;

K neschastyu, moya devochka,

K nam ne pridet rassvet.

Pozhaluysta, moya sladkaya,

Ne ukhodi, kogda

Ukhodyat veshi dorogie,

I ugasayet nadezhda.

Pomni, esli grustno,

Glavnoye, chto ya ponyal:

Beregi sebya, prosti sebya,

I podumay o tom, chto skazal:

Esli yest ogon,

      pust gorit.

Esli yest lyubov,

      ne day umeret.

U kovo yest vera?

      ne zabyvay;

I kto znaet Boga?

      Evo i umolyay.

Hope

A letter from a soldier to his lover, c. 1941, after the First Battle of Kiev

Today it seems to me,

There is no light in the sky;

Unfortunately, my dear,

Dawn is not coming to us.

Please, my sweetheart,

Do not leave when

Precious things go away

And all hope fades away.

Remember, if you are sad,
The main thing I understood:
Take care of yourself, forgive yourself,
And think of what I said:

If you have fire,
        let it burn.
If you have love,
        do not let it die.
Who has faith?
        do not forget it;
And who knows God?
        please, pray.

The Man in the Black Suit

"Where are we going?"

"We're going to see the man in the black suit."

"Doesn't he have a name?"

"No, he's just called the man in the black suit."

The curly-haired girl rested her head against the window as her mother drove along the straight and boring highway. An old car dealership stood in the gap between two fields. On its property was a condemned hovel, whose perpetually-collapsing front porch held ceiling-high stacks of tires.

"Wait on that porch," said the mother. The girl obeyed and watched quietly as she walked into the dealership. There was an arrangement of perfectly ordered cat bones beside her on the ground, though not a scrap of cat was left on them. It was as if a sorry feline had laid down to die, and the rest of the world simply let it be so. The girl found this to be a curious thing. She picked up a twig and tracing the skeletal remains in the dust, she managed to keep herself entertained for nearly five minutes. It was then that the man in the black suit approached her.

He tilted his head to the side, produced a small notepad from his pocket, and looked up again; this time even more confused than before. "Are you Susie Cartwright?"

The girl didn't look up. "Yessir. And I pr'sume you're the man in the black suit. Mommy told me we were goin'ta meet you today."

"By the looks of it, yes." He studied his notes again.

"How peculiar." He turned slightly, starting in the direction of the dealership, but had a second thought and instead took a seat next to Susie.

"You got a name, mister?" she asked.

"Not here."

"Why don't you pick one?"

The man in the black suit looked at the ground. "Well, I had a delicious plate of fries at Karen's Place this morning. How about you call me Karen?"

Susie burst into laughter. "But that's a girl's name!"

"Is that so? How funny. It will have to do." He extended his hand. "Hello, Susie, I am Karen."

The girl contained her giggles for just long enough to put on an English accent. "Good afternoon, Karen." She shook his hand. "Do you got a job?"

"Yes, I take people where they need to go. Some people come here of their own will, sometimes life drags them here, but mostly they're just brought. There's a man in that building who makes deals. For a price of some sort, they can bring someone to these old cat bones, and I'll come take them where they need to go. But it's usually old people, sad people, sick people, and mean people. I've never seen someone like you."

Susie set the twig down and folded her arms over her knees. "Why's that?"

"I don't know, Susie. Did your mother tell you why she brought you here?"

"No, sir. My mom's kinda cranky and she doesn't talk much. Ever since dad got her the divorce, she only talks 'bout how she'd be getting more checks in the mail if it wasn't for that stupid Henrietta Dwight. And the church ladies say its 'cause I'm not in school, which is fine by me 'cause I don't wanna be in school, but instead I always gotta pick switches. Do you gotta pick switches, too?"

"I'm not sure I know what that means. Does your mother make you do that often?"

"Oh, yes. She doesn't say nothing sometimes, she just gets real angry and points to the yard, and I gotta pick switches. I heard her talking on the telephone one time that she wishes Dad woulda tooken me with him to Fort Wayne. I don't know where's Fort Wayne. But Miss Blakely at church says it's just because she's a sad lady, but she loves me very much."

"I see." Karen looked at the sky and pondered for a few moments before returning to Susie and the conversation at hand. "I'm not exactly sure why you're here, but how about you come with me anyway?"

"Well, wher'ya goin'?"

"Mostly sad places, unfortunately. There

are plenty of those. But this world, and many other ones, have plenty of happy places, too. I do have a riverboat. Would you like to join me?"

"Do you have any wax bottles or ginger ale? I had those one time and they were pretty good."

"I suppose I could find some."

Susie picked up the twig again and peeled off the bark.

"Alright. I'll go."

The man in the black suit stood up, dusted himself off, and offered Susie a hand.

"Follow me," he said. "I promise everything is going to be okay."

In My Hands

In my hands, I hold the ocean-blue,
Like seas of darkness, they subdue;
And if I were the smallest fish,
I'd find a way to swim to you.

In my hands, I hold the skies above,
That carry crows, and larks, and doves;
And if the skies were like a box,
Still, they could not hold all my love.

My Jeannette, Immortal

My Jeannette, immortal, she lies,

Beyond the seas, beyond the skies,

Beyond the brightest fields of green,

Never unknown, but forever unseen.

Her soul remains among the trees,

Carrying the Nile's key.

She slips away from Death's cold grasp,

Forever free and safe at last.

Requiem No. 1

I remember dawn and afternoon,
I remember evening time;
When instead of sharply ceasing,
The sun would slowly hide.

I dream of dusk, sweet crimson dusk,
And pray to see its glow,
Instead, I find when I open my eyes:
Midnight's blackened throes.

I wait in the darkest hours of night,
When not a soul is near;
I grasp for words, I long to speak,
But no one remains to hear.

The Devil Drives A Black Volga

Once more, I beg for the hour to change,

But the clock—still—midnight reads;

I pray someday the sun will stay,

And blackness will recede.

A Call from Eugenie

There is a feeling you get when walking through a quiet park close to sundown: the wind kisses your skin, and the chills that follow alert you that you have somehow met that same wind before. It leaves as quickly as it came, but not before whispering, *I'll see you again soon*.

I liked to walk near the creek behind the ball park. Yes, it was an ugly creek. But the way it gently glistened reminded me of little crystals, like on the amateur radio my daughter liked to point out in the novelty store's window.

"The thing's so bedazzled it couldn't likely make a single contact!" my wife used to say. I thought she was probably right, but I still liked to assure little Eugenie that she could buy it if she saved the money.

We lived in Chicago, in the part of town where people could smell how much you made just by looking at you. We got all kinds of dirty looks when we walked past that novelty store, but we did our best to keep Eugenie distracted so she never felt lesser than the folks around her. Luckily, she was too young to understand the social consequences of being born to a store clerk and a courthouse custodian.

The trouble started coming after the war. An overzealous Truman saw fit to survey and examine all Federal employees to test their loyalty to the United States, lest a Soviet spy infiltrate a government institution. We thought we would be safe. The letter from the State Department addressed to Mr. and

Mrs. Arthur Pinch proved us wrong.

We complied to the letter's demands, leaving Eugenie with my wife's parents and promptly driving to Washington. Though we were promised high-quality, federal grade transportation to a discreet and simple loyalty interview, the windowless V-220 that carried us smelled of ammonia and the dusty hangar we soon arrived at seemed to swallow us whole.

"Did you know your husband's real name isn't Arthur Pinch?" I cringed as the Sergeant leaned closer to my wife. She shook her head. "Your husband," he pointed at me, "was born Artur Vitaliyevich Penchikov. What does that name sound like to you?" She said it sounded Russian. "Good girl!" he said. I cringed again. "Now, it's no crime to be Russian, is it, sweetheart? No, it's not. So why would your husband want to hide that from you?" She looked at me like she didn't know an answer, but she desperately wanted to. I looked away. I didn't like being here. I think you really begin to notice the ugliness of a room when you've been made uncomfortable in it. Or maybe all government buildings feel like that, because that's the state of a country after war.

I looked back at her. "Baby..." I didn't really know how to continue. She kept her eyes on me, but her mind must have been all over the place. "I just changed my name when I moved here... I was five years old... I promise I didn't know this would happen..." I realized then that I was rambling. I took off my hat so I'd have something to look at. "My mother didn't want me to have that kind of life."

The Sergeant laughed. "What kind of life, Penchikov? An immigrant's life?" He took my hat from my lap and examined it, smiling as he fiddled with the seams. "Well, maybe your mother should have thought about that before making you an immigrant." With a wave of his hand, my wife was escorted away. "Let's talk, alright?" he stared directly at me. "I think we can fix all of this."

He told me there would be a plane leaving for Yekaterinburg tomorrow morning. No, I won't get to see my wife or daughter again. And I shouldn't think about leaving the building, he said, or else they'll muster up some kind of federal offense to pin on me. Something about fraud and resisting arrest. I didn't care; the large men blocking the exit seemed to pose more of a threat to me than legal trouble, anyway.

I remember the airport being cold the next morning, but the cabin of the plane was uncomfortably hot. I felt glad when it started to rain. Perhaps the temperature would drop in the sun's absence.

An hour passed, and then two. The rain beat relentlessly on the aircraft's shell. I found myself missing the sunshine, as its warm rays would have provided a nice hug through my window. I rested my head on the glass regardless. It was cold. It felt like death.

I was soon startled awake as a blinding flare split the sky, followed by a resounding crash. Those unintelligible noises of concern arose from the seats around me. The whole plane sounded like a wife asking her husband, "What's going on?" to which he would respond, "How the heck would I know?"

They sat like nervous stalks of celery until the loudest crash of them all rumbled them out of their seats. The man sitting closest to the window faced the mob forming around him, saying, "We've been hit!" The noises of concern turned quickly to noises of horror.

It felt like plummeting at first, but then cascading, and then merely descending. We descended in disturbing peace for longer than one would think, until with a jolt our vessel confronted the ground. Tree limbs pierced the aisle, goring some who had not been crushed by luggage and ceiling panels.

And then it was black. The darkness hit me like a punch in the stomach. I was silent but aching and agonizing all over, lying in vast nothingness. There were no thoughts, no dialogue with the self; only quiet neural processes that told me that the only thing I knew of what was going on is that it hurt.

Then, like a seal being broken, my eyelids parted, and I was able to see. It looked like a waiting room, but it didn't smell very medical. It was pleasant. The man sitting across from me nudged his friend.

"Hey, hey Fred, he's awake!" Fred slowly opened his eyes. He seemed to have dozed off.

"Huh? Oh, yeah." He looked at his watch. "I got six minutes exactly."

"Six minutes!" Fred's friend looked at me. "You sore, buddy?"

"Yeah, a little bit." That was the truth. Most of the pain had left me, but some tenseness in my arms and legs lingered. "Say, where are we, fellas?"

"Funny if we know. I'm Bill. This is Fred. We just got here thirty minutes ago. Think they're fillin' out paperwork or somethin'."

I shook their hands. "Arthur Pinch."

"Is there an Artur Penchikov here?" called a lady at the front desk.

"That works too," I nodded to Fred and Bill. I reached to tip my hat but realized that the Sergeant had never given it back.

I approached the desk, where two fake blonde ladies looked up at me over their glasses. "You sore, Mister?" one asked. "I bet he's sore. He's been through it."

"Just a little bit, ma'am," I responded. "What's that ringing?"

"It's just the strangest thing! See that sparkly ham radio over there?" I nodded. There were lots of ham radios behind the desk, but only one was sparkly and ringing. "It's been going crazy ever since you got here!"

"These aren't normal radios," said the other woman. "They work just like telephones; they ring, you pick 'em up, talk; no fancy stuff. Except the signal's stronger because it's a radio. Everybody who walks through this room gets their own. They get one call to the other side, and that's it."

"Oh, Edith, you're making us sound like a prison again," said the first woman. She gave me a reassuring look. "You're not in prison. Go see who's trying to reach you."

I approached the ringing, bejeweled apparatus, and picked up the receiver. "Hello?"

***

"Mommy! Guess who it is!"

The slender woman rested her broom against the doorframe and stood next to her young daughter. "Who is it?"

The girl's voice dropped to a whisper.

"Listen!" She handed the receiver to her mother.

"Honey, I don't hear anything."

"What do you mean? It's Dad!"

She stared at the girl for a few seconds. "It most certainly isn't."

"Wait, just listen again!"

The woman picked up her broom. "Just five more minutes with that thing, and then you need to go to bed."

The girl returned to her conversation. "Hey, guess what, Grandma bought me that sparkly radio! And guess what I'm using right now! Yeah! Where did you go to?"

***

"I'm just a little bit far away right now, sweetie. It's all going to be okay."

"Okay," said the voice on the other end. "I'll see you again soon."

"Follow me, Mr. Penchikov," Edith rose and moved towards the door. "We'll get you a new hat."

On This Crooked Path, Madness Lies

DARYA VYAZOVA, LISTVYANKA.
TO SOFIA YULYEVNA WITTE, MOSCOW.
18 JANUARY, 1906

DEAREST MADAME WITTE,

I thank you with unfeigned candor in regards to your work in Moscow. I hope your brother is well, and can also receive my sincere gratitude. I do believe our dear Sergei has outdone himself in his railroad endeavours. I have sent with this letter a parcel containing ancient water from Lake Baikal. Please ensure it is delivered safely to

Sergei, and that he is aware of my warm sentiments concerning the new Circum-Baikal railway that would not have been completed without his efforts. I apologize if this matter brings you any trouble. I am sure you remember the times when I could simply write to him myself, but now that his name bears the illustrious title—Chairman of the Council of Ministers —how glorious! I fear my letters would be lost in all of his official papers.

In my own work, I remain indefatigable. The schoolhouse was completed last month, and my words cannot adequately convey the wealth of opportunities birthed by this Eastern diaspora! It is all in the railway, dear Sofia. I have met businessmen from Moscow and Saint Petersburg; they are all moving here because of these railway towns. I taught fifteen students today, six of them brand-new. Please hasten your reply! I miss

Moscow terribly and wait expectantly to hear from you.

Sincerely,

Darya Vyazova

***

SOFIA WITTE, MOSCOW.
TO DARYA VYAZOVA, LISTVYANKA.
8 FEBRUARY, 1906.

MY DEAR FRIEND,

All is well in Moscow! My brother was delighted to receive the lake-water, which he calls the purest bottle of crystalline liquid he has ever seen. He has set it proudly on his shelf amongst his finest plum-brandies. He would write to you himself if he was not so mired in this horrid political fiasco of recent times. Please, tell me more of your school-house! I apologize that my letters may be short- I am hard at work with the Women's League.

With Love,

Sofia Witte

***

DARYA VYAZOVA, LISTVYANKA.
TO SOFIA YULYEVNA WITTE, MOSCOW.
1 MARCH, 1906.

DARLING SOFIA,

I have heard news of the Women's League already! How proud I am- both of your own accomplishments and your brother's railroad! Ah, how quickly does news travel by train! My dear, you have done such great things in Moscow that I can barely acquiesce in the discussion of my meager school-house. Though, I will say- things are beautiful here! The crisp shore of the Baikal—how it cuts through those grand evergreen hills like a rock-carven blade of azure and foam. I do miss life in the city, but how serene it is in Listvyanka! I beseech you to visit me soon, but perhaps you will not wish to return to Moscow! My fifteen students have grown to twenty. Things are most lovely here!

 Yours,

 Dasha

***

SOFIA WITTE, MOSCOW.
TO DARYA VYAZOVA, LISTVYANKA.
22 MARCH, 1906

 MY DEAR DARUSHKA,

 What joy to receive your letters! My deepest sorrow is that I cannot write more.

 Always yours,

 Sofia

***

DARYA VYAZOVA, LISTVYANKA.
TO SOFIA YULYEVNA WITTE, MOSCOW.
26 APRIL, 1906

 DEAR SOFIA,

 I apologize for my leave, for I have been most busy. My students have increased from twenty to twenty-seven.

For this I am grateful, but we have run out of desks and many of them must stand against the wall. We are packed very tightly in this small room. I must tell you something, Sofia. I have grown concerned about the state of things. There is a deep and wide river flowing here—the Angara (which feeds from the Yenisey)—it pours into Lake Baikal and they meet right on the shores of our town. Its waters move from the earth, therefore it never freezes over and it drives itself quickly. But Sofia, I have not seen its current move this year. There are no tides to lap the rocks. The water that reaches the shore is so frightfully stagnant. Oh, how I talk like an old woman. Please be patient with me. I do not heed superstition—but there is more. Young Alyona Shupina has fallen ill with a spring fever. I fear it is spreading in the school-house, and I have been examining the children's arms for bruises and their mouths for bleeding. I found what may have been a small hemorrhage on Inna Olesovna's gums, so I sent her and her brother home at once. I watched them from the window as they made their way down the path to the village. Inna fell to the ground before she was even a quarter-mile away, and her brother Dima came running back to the schoolhouse. His face was wet with tears as he told me what he thought had become of his sister. I sent two older girls, Raisa and Nadya, to walk them to the doctor. My dear Sofia, I fear for what may become of this spring fever. Such a thing brings chaos to children in small quarters. On this crooked path, madness lies.

Keep me ever in your consideration,
Darya

***

DARYA VYAZOVA, LISTVYANKA.
TO SOFIA YULYEVNA WITTE, MOSCOW.
3 MAY, 1906.

MY DEAREST SOFYUSHKA,

I wish not to hasten you, though my matters are urgent. The Angara produced a putrid stench shortly after I wrote to you. Dead fish washed up on the banks, and the whole river looked brown and murky. Never in my time here have I witnessed such a distasteful thing. Not long after that, a most peculiar storm found us. It snows as I write, though it is May! Three more children are sick at home. My dread takes deeper root by the hour.

Remember me, and write!

Darya

***

DARYA VYAZOVA, LISTVYANKA.
TO SOFIA YULYEVNA WITTE, MOSCOW.
10 MAY, 1906.

SOFIA,

I have received word that there are

now no trains leaving Listvyanka, and no mail is to be carried. We are all stuck in this horrid, horrid place. I pray to God that my letters may reach you soon, and I will persist in my writing until the dawn of such a day. Please, if you read this, send for Sergei! We need his wisdom now more than ever.

With love, though I am afraid,

Your dear Dasha

***

DASHA VYAZOVA, LISTVYANKA.
TO SOFIA YULYEVNA WITTE, MOSCOW.
15 MAY, 1906.

SOFIA,

The temperatures today dropped below negative fifteen degrees Celsius. A messenger came from the village telling us to keep within the school-house until the weather improved. Word had come from an Eastern town that an even harsher blizzard was due us. We are now approaching five hours locked in the school-house, and I fear this may be the last of my letters to you. At exactly midday, the youngest of my pupils began to tremble in her seat. Her shakes became so violent that even her chair and desk rattled with her, and she dropped her pencils and gripped her face. Another student cried out in horror upon running to the window. The snow had blurred the horizon like a thick and eerie mist, and all vision was obscured in the vast white. Alas, emerging from the haze were six dark figures on horses, drawing close and then disappearing before anything more than their silhouettes could be perceived. The young boy at the window began to tremble like the first girl, and then another, and then a third. Soon, nearly half of the children shook uncontrollably on the floor.

"What is that scratching on the walls?" cried one sound student. "What is the tapping at the door?" cried another.

Those who were not shaking were overcome with fear on account of mysterious sounds outside the school. Suddenly, without a word or warning, one boy arose and pierced another with his pencil just before collapsing with him and holding the bleeding classmate. "He told me to! He told me to!" he exclaimed amid tears. This ignited a panic: the students gored with pencils, shattered writing slates over heads, and some broke windows and plunged into the snowbanks. I ran after them, but their limbs were twisted and necks broken from diving head-first. There were, but four children left conscious in the school. I sustained punctures in my legs and arms as students attempted to attack me with glass-shards upon my re-entry to the building. I have, at this point, locked myself in a coat closet where I write to you hopelessly. I still hear screams from the outside- there are at least two children left. But there are voices I do not recognize as well, and heavy footsteps. Now, as I write, they scratch at the door and laugh. I do not know how much longer

This collection has been archived by the Department for Protecting the Public Security and Order, courtesy of Listvyanka Board of Education and municipal government.

The Iconoclasm of the Aeolist

The life of a man holds both gladness and
gloom,
Through both joy and through pain he must
go;
But all of this joy has been stolen from me,
By Eudora Ann Munro.

When I was a boy, I was all alone,
Far from me my classmates would hide;
Both teachers and students were terrified of
me,
On account of my troubled mind.

But along came a girl with eyes of green,

Whose name was Eudora Munro;
She was sweet, she was kind, she was
wonderful then,
But that was many years ago.

I worked a whole year just to build her a
house,
A house west of Sailor Springs;
But she'd sold her soul to her Catholic
Church,
And to candles and holy things.

All night and all day, I dreamed of Eudora,
In my house by the river's firth;
She was a woman too holy for Hades,
indeed;
But a demon too wicked for Earth.

She spoke nothing but prayers, and I hated
her prayers,
To Saint Paul and to Saint Lucía;
I hated the sound of her self-righteous

praise,

Her hymns and her Ave Marias.

But on one fateful day, the sound left my
ears,

Her psalms I could hear no more;

From then on I no longer hated her song,

But I hated the oath that she swore.

This was an oath that dressed her in black,

And forced her to move far away;

Her oath kept her locked in a convent,

Where she would live for the rest of her days.

I hated this more than I ever did hate,

And my hatred caused me to surmise;

That Eudora must pay for the pain she has
caused,

And her religion must pay for its crimes.

On blackened nights with troubled skies,

I devised my wicked plan;

The Devil Drives A Black Volga

I dreamt of all the wicked ways
To end Eudora Ann.

Then appeared on the horizon-line:
A glow, a billow of smoke;
And deep within my soul I felt,
My true plan had been evoked.

With the rising of the morning sun,
I hurried into town;
And I bought a box of matches,
To burn the convent down.

By train I journeyed to the north,
Till I reached the monastic home;
I trembled not as I lit a match,
For my presence was unknown.

As I stepped away, the flames arose,
And scaled the smoke-stained wall;
Fiery jewels cascaded to earth,
Ash and embers began to fall.

I gazed in awe at the marvelous blaze,
My revenge! What a glorious sight!
But then from the cloister a clamor arose,
Piercing the smoky night.

A shriek emerged from the building in
flames,
And after that shriek expired,
Another shriek rose, this one worse than the
first,
One by one, they discovered the fire.

Headlong I fell, in horrified shock,
I clenched my ears until from them flowed
blood;
I tore out my hair and I joined with the
screams,
As my terror drowned me in its flood.

I lifted my head, for I heard something new,
My ears had retrieved a new sound;

More than the wails, this sound terrified me:
The sound of footsteps rumbling the ground.

"Be gone!" I screamed, but the steps
faltered not,
I shouted, but only in vain;
"A life for a life!" cried the seraphs above,
Pouring scorn on my soul in disdain.

Now a gallow-tree stands in the center of
town,
As an omen, horrid and tall;
There I shall hang, and meet my cruel fate,
To be loathed and detested by all.

Idris's Chair

INTERVIEWER: Mr. Henry Frazier

SUBJECT: Mr. James Sarafin

TIME: 1:00 PM

DATE: December 18, 1901

LOCATION: Office of the Chicago Tribune, Chicago, Ill.

FRAZIER: Good afternoon, Mister Sarafin. [Motions to chair] Please have a seat.

SARAFIN: Good afternoon, sir. [sits down]

FRAZIER: Please state your name and age for the public record.

SARAFIN: James Sarafin, aged twenty-nine.

FRAZIER: Thank you, sir. As you know, the topic of this interview is your recent Trans-Atlantic expedition to Wales. Please tell, what was the purpose of this journey?

SARAFIN: I, along with two companions, traveled to Snowdonia to endeavor to climb the great Cadair Idris. Many a myth and legend have been told of this mountain, which you have likely heard.

FRAZIER: (:☺ I fear not, Mister Sarafin.
SARAFIN: The local Welshmen believe in a great giant of old, Idris. The mountain is his chair, "cadair" in their native tongue. It is said that if a man reaches the top of the mountain, one of three outcomes will be prescribed unto him; the most favorable being that he will be given all wisdom known in Heaven and Earth. However, if Idris beholds him without favour, the man may

be put to death instantly. Even worse, he could succumb to madness.

FRAZIER: And you, sir? What do you believe?

SARAFIN: First, you must know that the original intentions for my expedition were merely geographical. I had quite the interest in mapping the region. We stayed in a village for a few nights in preparation for the hike, and upon hearing the Welshmen's rumours-

FRAZIER: I am terribly sorry to interrupt, sir, but what rumours?

SARAFIN: The villagers told us of explorers who attempted to hike the mountain before us. Many have never returned. There were still a few who survived, but no one would dare tell us what became of them.

FRAZIER: Thank you for elaborating, sir. Pardon my interruption. Please continue.

SARAFIN: After hearing these rumours, we became curious. None of us, save Fransen, were believers of religion or conspiracy, but we listened to their talk in the spirit of inquiry. Within days, we three pragmatics began our trek with a new mindset.

FRAZIER: I suppose my question was, have you maintained your pragmatism?

SARAFIN: The answer you seek is more than merely a yes or no. I must recount my entire tale to you if you are truly curious.

FRAZIER: Of course, sir. The public is eager to know what happened on the mountain.

SARAFIN: It took merely a day to get to the peak. We left immediately after break-fast, and stopped only once for lunch. Upon reaching the top, we built a fire, had supper, and rested. We saw or heard nothing out of the ordinary. In factuality, we all had quite the laugh about our previous curiosity, determining the myth to be false. But when I awoke in the morning, Fransen remained slumbering. I crept over to where he lay, perhaps to mock the old Swede, but not even shouting woke him. The giant man was lying on his stomach, so I decided to turn him over as my concern grew. His eyes were not closed, but wide open, like he had been frozen.

FRAZIER: Frozen in ice, sir? Did he succumb to hypothermia?

SARAFIN: No, not ice! Frozen he was, but somehow untouched by anything that would give evidence for his ending. He was simply motionless, with his last expression still remaining on his face. It was the strangest sight. For I have seen the dead before, Mister Frazier, but I have doubts that any man has seen what I saw that morning.

FRAZIER: Have you any idea what killed him?

SARAFIN: Not any you would believe! There was no evidence, like I said, none at all! We knew, or at least I knew, that no cause for his death was likely to ever be found. So, for this reason, I buried Mister Fransen on the top of the mountain, all on my own.

FRAZIER: But what of your other companion, Mister Mezenski? Where was he?

SARAFIN: Therein lies a curiosity. He was nowhere to be found. There were footprints leading down the trail, and though I was confused, I supposed he had already begun the journey back to the village.

FRAZIER: Have you not found or contacted him since the expedition?

SARAFIN: I have not, though I was informed of his arrival in the U.S. shortly after mine. It was a mere telegram, however, containing no specific information pertinent to his well-being. Have you any of this information, sir?
FRAZIER: In fact, I do. I believe Mister Mezenski has returned to Cook County, but has remained solely in the confines of his home.

SARAFIN: (::) I see.

FRAZIER: Yes. Now, allow me to redirect us to my question from earlier. Have your experiences on the mountain brought forth changes to your personal views of superstition?

SARAFIN: In more common circumstances, I

would ridicule such a question. But I fear something has changed in me. While I lay awake on that mountaintop, I pondered the stories told by the villagers. What if we were to die, or lose our minds? When I awoke and found the deceased Fransen, my worries intensified. What if, instead of sharing the same fate, each one of us was given a different outcome from the three? I reasoned that since death had been claimed, I must now be very wise or very mad. Then came the dreadful thought. Mezenski left us because he felt instantly wiser when he awoke. When he saw Fransen was dead, he reasoned that I must have contracted the insanity, and fled to protect himself.

FRAZIER: Do you (::) feel mad, sir?

SARAFIN: Of course I don't *feel* mad. No one does, especially not madmen. (::) The fact that I have *felt* no change is a primary reason for my concern. For if I have grown wise, surely I would feel it. But it is the most deranged killers who normalize their thoughts in their own minds. (:::) There have been other factors contributing to my theory. As I walked the trail leading down the mountain, [glances briefly around room] I believe I heard things, things that were not really there. For instance, I heard footsteps, and even voices on occasion, but there was no one around. [Looking at window] (:::) I have been prone to disquietude in these recent days. Lack of sleep, sweating, outbursts of terror triggered by random occurrences... aren't those all symptoms of madness? Do I speak like a madman?

FRAZIER: Perhaps you are correct about your symptoms, but I find you to be speaking rather clearly. As a matter of fact, Mister Sarafin, you have answered every question I have for you. Unless you have more to say, sir?

SARAFIN: No, Mister Frazier. Thank you.

FRAZIER: Thank you for your time, sir. [BOTH RISE]
[END OF INTERVIEW]

***

INTERVIEWER: Mr. Henry Frazier
SUBJECT: Mr. Frederic Mezenski
TIME: 3:30 PM DATE: December 18, 1901
LOCATION: Office of the Chicago Tribune, Chicago, Ill.

FRAZIER: Thank you for coming, Mister Mezenski. Please have a seat.
MEZENSKI: [sits down] [whispers unintelligibly]

FRAZIER: I'm sorry, but if you're talking to me, I can't understand you.

MEZENSKI: [continues whispering] [shivers

suddenly and brushes something off
shoulder]

FRAZIER: Is everything alright?

MEZENSKI: You've got to fix your roof, sir.

FRAZIER: Is there an issue with it?

MEZENSKI: It's leaking, see? [takes off
suitcoat] Got my coat all wet. [whispers
more]

FRAZIER: (:::) I see. (::) May I ask what you're
whispering?

MEZENSKI: [motions toward stenographer]
Not if she's going to type it down.

FRAZIER: I promise it will be off the record.

MEZENSKI: I don't want anybody to know.

FRAZIER: Nobody will know.

MEZENSKI: I was just counting.

FRAZIER: Counting? (::) Counting what?

MEZENSKI: Mister Fransen told me to count.

FRAZIER: When?

MEZENSKI: He got scared on the mountain that he was going to die, so he told me to count with him until he dies so he's not as scared, but he never told me to stop counting. So I'm still counting.

FRAZIER: (::) What number are you on, sir?

MEZENSKI: Two hundred thousand, sixty seven.

FRAZIER: Have you been sleeping?

MEZENSKI: I don't sleep. I just count.

FRAZIER: (::) Of course, sir. (::) Could you tell me from your perspective what happened on the mountain?

MEZENSKI: (::::) FRAZIER: Sir?

MEZENSKI: What about it?

FRAZIER: I suppose I'm specifically asking for your opinion on the Welsh mythology that Mister James Sarafin told me about. MEZENSKI: What'd he tell you?

FRAZIER: He told me about the giant and the possibility of three fates. I want merely your unbiased opinion. Do you feel any different after returning from the mountain?

MEZENSKI: (::) Yes. I do.

FRAZIER: Is that all? (::) Just different? Do you feel madder? Or wiser? STENOGRAPHER: Do you understand the question, Mister Mezenski?

MEZENSKI: [staring at stenographer] (::) Do I understand? Of course, I understand. You, I believe, you are the one who does not understand. [looks back at Frazier] I am the wisest man on Earth. [pointing at stenographer] Does she know that? Does she know that, Mister Frazier? [rises] [walks to stenographer's desk]

FRAZIER: Wait a minute, Mister Mezenski, why don't you sit down and tell me more about being the wisest man on Earth?

MEZENSKI: [to stenographer] You don't understand, madam. You don't understand what I'm capable of. My knowledge and understanding extends far past your very plane of existence. You don't—

FRAZIER: Please, sir, sit down—

MEZENSKI: [pointing at Frazier, trembling] Quiet! [back to stenographer] I'm done with you, [looking at Frazier] and I'm done with him. [retrieves coat from chair] It would be in your best interests not to publish this interview. [walks toward door]

FRAZIER: Is that a threat?
MEZENSKI: [mumbling] [slams door]
[END OF INTERVIEW]

***

December 24, 1901
From the desk of Henry Frazier:

A few days have passed since my interviewing of Messrs. Sarafin and Mezenski.

Several peculiarities in the case have prompted me to do research of my own. I first met with friends and relatives of Mister Sarafin, who all presented me with the same startling responses. James Sarafin did not journey to Snowdonia for geographical purposes. Much to my surprise, he had no collegiate degree or high school diploma. Prior to the expedition, Sarafin was a construction worker in downtown Chicago with no interest in geography whatsoever. As for his true motives for the journey, no one knows. His associates noticed a stark contrast in his behaviour after his return. He told his wife that he felt his mind had capitulated to insanity. He was promptly referred to a psychiatrist, who diagnosed him with the severest case of neurasthenia he had ever seen. Mister James Sarafin passed away on Wednesday from cardiac arrest due to fatal arrhythmia. It was like the weight of the entire world was placed on his shoulders, and he collapsed from the pressure.

I was also given the opportunity to interview the associates of Mister Frederic Mezenski. His wife claims he never returned home after the expedition but instead rented an apartment in the downtown area and ignored all calls and telegrams. He was admitted to the Cook County Insane Asylum after being diagnosed with severe schizophrenia and psychosis.

I suppose, after reviewing my findings, I have concluded one thing. Mister Sarafin *felt* that he was going crazy, while he was quite possibly the wisest man on Earth. Mister Mezenski's situation was the exact inverse. Perhaps there is a mythical giant in Wales, and perhaps not; but I now know there was something— something so extraordinary and magnificent that would cause each man to forsake their own nature, even to adopt a new brand of existence.

Afternoon Tea

Would you enjoy some afternoon tea?
With thyme, we'll drink a cup or three.
Frilly dresses we shall wear,
With golden flowers in our hair.

While dancing in the cool summer breeze,
We'll run away so secretly.
To the forest, we shall go,
For to build our cottage-home.

Like sprites and leprechauns in the mist,
We'll pick up leaves the sun hath kissed.
Rocks and gemstones we'll collect,
For jewelry to adorn our necks.

And lastly, when the fair sun hath hid,

A sweet farewell we two shall bid.

But you and I shall both agree:

We'd rather drink more afternoon tea.

Where There Is a
Cold, Dark Cave

Where there is a cold, dark cave,

There is a place to hide until you are found

By something that is big

And hungry.

I walked the Earth when it was new.

There were Flying Things and Crawling

Things,

But we Walking Things were most feared of

all.

For every Walking Thing on Earth desired

only to kill

But to live, too.
And the entire world was terrified.

The Walking Things were people like us,
But they were not human.
In humans there is evil, but also good;
There is restraint.
There is hesitation before drawing blood
from your brother.
The Walking Things were not human.

My father was a teacher in this time,
When Walking Things were their own gods.
They spared my father's life only because his
teachings humored them.

He taught of death.
He taught of an end to all Walking Things—
A vengeance from Heaven.

He taught of mighty waters soon to come,
But there are no mighty waters in the desert.

He taught of the final days,
But there are no final days for gods.
And the Walking Things mocked him.

He built a Vessel large enough for all
Walking Things,
And many Flying Things and Crawling Things.
But the Walking Things despised the Vessel.
There was no need for such a thing in such a
place.

At least,
Not until the sky grew dark.

And when the sky grew dark, the clouds
burst open.
When the clouds burst open, the mountains
broke,
And from them flowed waters dark and
deep.

For once, the Walking Things were not

terrified of each other,
But of God.

There in the hills was a cold, dark cave.
Many could not fit in the cave, and were
swept away by the waters
As they stood wailing from the outside.

The waters were big,
And they were hungry.
Those in the cave could see the Vessel from
a distance. They knew the cave could not
spare them for much longer.

There were strong reeds nearby—
Strong enough to hold the weight of many
men.
They gathered them all together and tied
knots.
One particularly fearsome Walking Thing
presented himself to brave the waters,
To swim near the Vessel,

And to cast the reeds aboard so that many
others would be saved.

And so he did;
I watched as he swam a great distance,
As he propelled himself above the water to
gather the hand-made rope,
As he cast it into the air with but a few
shallow breaths in his lungs,

And I watched as the rope brushed against
the side of the Vessel and sank into the
deep.
He cried loudly in anguish,
And I watched from my window as he sank
with the rope.

It was then that the many remaining
Walking Things realized
That their final chance of salvation was
upon themselves.

J. Elmore

I saw fathers leave their sobbing wives,
Mothers abandon their screaming children;
The strongest first, with the weak ones left
behind;
They all came and threw themselves against
the walls of the Vessel.

They pleaded loudly for their lives,
But my father could not hear them.
They continued to scream and cry out
against my father for many hours that day,
But soon it was silent.

And there came a day that not even a bird
could we hear from the outside.
And it was silent for many days.
I remember most clearly when on the day
the Vessel found land
We stepped out into the place we
expected to know,
 But there was nothing we knew in this new
world.

There were no leaves on the trees,
And everything was browned with mud and
clay.

Worst of all was the stench,
Which found us before we even opened the
door.
Vast and harrowing fields of millions and
millions of bones
Lay spread out as far as one could see.

And I looked upon the bones of those I
once knew,
Some Walking Things, some Crawling Things,
And I remembered how my life meant
nothing more.
I remembered the lives I took,
The evil I have done with my own hands,
And I saw myself as those muddy bones
around me.

I still remember the very last time I watched

a man die.

That time, there was no knife in my hand,

But I watched from a window and was

silent.

Even now, though I am old,

I remember my father, who God alone

called just.

I hesitated before stepping onto the Vessel,

But he ushered me forward and pleaded

with me to not turn back.

Oh, how I wonder what a world you would

live in,

If he had turned away, and with the masses,

Had laughed at God?

On Broken Limbs Would I Cross the Stars

On broken limbs would I cross the stars,

For another soul to find;

With fractured hands, would I reach from where

My own soul is confined.

My muted tongue and silenced lips

No longer would restrain;

Till only you, and only I,

Forever would remain.

The Note in the Corridor

As I arose one morning in my opulent
chateau,
I, the King, did revel in my land that lies
below.
I gazed upon the fields and trees, and quiet
riverbeds,
Then turned away and placed my golden
crown upon my head.

I proceeded from my bedroom to my
empty corridor,
Where I found a note had drifted to the
stony floor:

"Look on my deeds, ye kings of old!
Beware my works and fear—
The future of thy kingdom
Lies in thine, and thine is here!"

Aghast, I dropped the page and ran to find
what had been done,
I feared some wicked villain must have stol'n
my only son!

I hurried 'round the chambers, searching for
him everywhere,
Upon entering his room, I found he was still
lying there.
I was truly quite relieved to know my son was
not with them,
For it seemed the lowly robbers stole my
daughter 'stead of him.

I retired to my chamber, and I closed and
locked my door,

And I slept, knowing the matter wouldn't plague me anymore.

鹬 先 生

我叫鹬先生。

曾经飞，今不能。

男人偷去我的膀子，

所以我吃他的孩子。

Shuì Xiānshēng

Wǒ jiào shuì xiānshēng.

Céngjīng fēi, jīn bùnéng.

Nánrén tōu qù wǒ de bǎngzi,

Suǒyǐ wǒ chī tā de háizi.

Mr. Owl

My name is Mr. Owl.

I used to fly; now, I cannot.

A man stole my wing.

Now I will eat his child.

Vodyanoy

The Vodyanoy are a species of malevolent creatures that inhabit the rivers of Eastern Europe. Some legends have recorded them as fish-like, while in others, they possess amphibious qualities. At their most benign, they are sometimes willing to strike deals with desperate humans. Vigilance is of utmost importance, however, because the bloodthirsty creatures often drown their victims.

Vodyanoy, vodyanoy, who live in the deep,

Rise to the surface to answer my plea.

To answer my plea, or my prayer instead;

Please help me survive, for my husband is
dead.

There is no one to work if my husband is
dead,
And if no work is done, there will be no more
bread.
If there is no more bread for my children to
eat,
There will be fewer workers to harvest the
wheat.

If the wheat is not gleaned and brought into
town,
The food we are storing will quickly run out.
If there is no more food to be stored in our
bins,
There will be no more food for our fighting
men.

If our men have no food, they'll be too
weak to fight,

And defend our Rossíya from treacherous
plights.
Then if upon us a grim plight would fall,
Our rival could easily capture us all.

When everyone else has been captured,
save thee,
Your kingdom will sink to the depths of your
sea.
Alone in the rivers, alone you shall be-
For your sake, vodyanoy, please liberate
me.

The Parador Ariston Files

Subject was instructed to detail the circumstances leading her to Mar del Plata, Argentina.

I was born in Washington. I remember it was very cold. My father was a researcher dealing with the sea levels at Puget Sound. I don't remember much about that. His job moved him eventually to Argentina, to where we gladly accompanied him, because we didn't care for the cold.

I remember how different things were back then; how exciting and familiar the sea felt to me as a child. I didn't feel like I moved to a different country, but simply from a cold ocean to a warmer one. There was a sweet emptiness about the area. There were fewer cargo ships and more sailboats. There were no condominiums but many fishing shacks. It wasn't a city back then, or at least I wouldn't call it that; but a small cluster of homes that sort of lined the shore. The rest of it, where the skyscrapers are now, was very vast and grassy.

Roberta—my sister—and I used to sit on the cliffs and throw rocks at seagulls. I don't think we meant any harm except for Roberta, who was five years old and full of malice. She passed away last year, unfortunately, and I don't believe she remembered anything about Washington.

Now that I think about it, we were never meant to stay in Argentina. I think it was a three- or five-year arrangement. But my mother died after the first year, and I understand now how difficult it would have been for my father to return to Washington without her. So, we never left.

Subject was instructed to recall how she became involved with Filipe Quiroga.

I met him in my final year of secondary school. He always made a point to express how menial and useless his studies were- in fact, he dropped out before the year was over because he believed he had what it took to be a film director. We had begun going out at that point, against my father's will, so I tried to convince him to consider a stabler industry. Of course, he would not listen to me. He always told me he could make me a star like Isa Romano (though I had no acting experience), which sounds more than ideal to any seventeen-year-old girl.

That's what he told me on the day he proposed. He had a big plan of founding a film studio in Mar del Plata, of making great films to surpass the notoriety of the American ones; and I quite honestly enjoyed the uncertainty of the whole situation. I married him shortly after graduation.

Subject was instructed to detail the circumstances under which she became involved with the Parador Ariston.

My husband proved unsuccessful as a director, to say the least. I remember his first film. He wrote letters to seven possible producers, but the only two that responded rejected him harshly. Again, he had good ideas, and when he explained his plots and casting to me, it all seemed so vivid and brilliant. But little did I know, he was barely literate. His scripts were absolutely awful. It was just failure after failure, honestly. He'd finally snag a deal but would lose funding immediately when the producer-to-be saw the state of his writing and organization. He finally gave up after five long years. I had to wait tables during that time to make barely enough for us to live on.

That's when things started really changing in Mar del Plata- the government wanted to gentrify the coast and get more money from real estate. Do you remember Marcel Breuer? He was an architect from Europe back then, a really fancy type. Well, somehow, they managed to hire him for a building project—a rich people's club right on the same cliffs Roberta and I used to play on. Word got around, and all the businessmen in town wanted some piece of it.

Now, I didn't know this, but my husband had gotten involved with some characters around that time. Two of the gambling kinds, Mauricio Avila and Bruno Casas; I think he was trying to get them to lend him money for a film at some point. They played cards together a lot. Mauricio's uncle was the mayor, and he got to speak with Marcel and the other project leaders personally. That's because Mauricio was his favorite nephew. The mayor was able to talk all the builders and financiers into giving him a ginormous share in the business, which he gave all of to Mauricio, and this was a share large enough essentially to make someone an owner. I think that's where Bruno came in. He somehow convinced Mauricio he couldn't handle owning a business, and he needed help from the other two. They decided to split the share evenly and all three became co-owners.

Subject was instructed to detail the sequence of events surrounding the incident on February 27, 1948.

First of all, my husband was a good man. Even Mauricio was a good man. They were just foolish. They were school friends, you know; they got into gambling back then for fun and they never got out of it. Now, Bruno, he was shady. I didn't know Filipe was involved with him until it was too late. I never would have allowed it.

Bruno was very addicted to cocaine. He was part of a notorious ring from Buenos Aires, but he was under an agreement that he would never bring it into dealings with Filipe and Mauricio. By the time he had gotten in with the Ariston, however, he was very, very addicted. He was also the worst gambler of the bunch. He started investing unbelievable amounts of his personal money in the club, so much more than the other two would have invested. I think he wanted more control. That alone irritated my husband.

In addition to that, he started inviting unapproved guests to meet at the club even before its official opening, and to a greater extent after the opening. The club was often full of Bruno's cocaine buddies. It was beginning to earn a bad name from that. The last straw was the week before the 27th, when Mauricio and Filipe found out that the extra money he had been investing was comprised entirely of his dirty cocaine money. Filipe planned on simply dropping out of the agreement, but Mauricio was furious.

The Ariston was set to host a birthday party that Friday for actress Isa Romano. Though it was a well-kept secret, Isa had bought from the ring in the past. Her connections to Bruno and his friends, though private, were what allowed her such a lavish celebration.

All was going smoothly besides the very obvious tension in the air. About halfway into the party, however, Bruno began to act very strange, and I decided to keep my eyes on him. He looked nervously around the room, staring directly at Mauricio time and again, and I noticed how his foot tapped almost painfully fast, and his profuse sweating was nearly drenching his shirt. At one point, he trembled so violently that his table shook. Even Isa was distracted by his odd behavior. Suddenly, he gripped his chest, cried out, and collapsed sideways out of his chair. The woman sitting next to him checked his pulse and promptly called for the bartender to phone the hospital.

Bruno was pronounced dead. They called it acute cocaine poisoning. The party ended early, but we were all asked to stay to talk to police.

Subject was instructed to describe the aftermath of the incident.

Mauricio secretly met with his uncle, who was, as always, sympathetic to his case. He paid off the cops and had the papers call it a heart attack. Filipe, on the other hand, felt uneasy about brushing the situation under the rug, and he had a plan to report what he knew to the authorities and catch a boat to Uruguay (with me, of course). We had our bags packed to leave on March 4th , but my husband did not wake up that morning after suffering the same kind of "heart attack" as Bruno.

I never returned to the Parador Ariston. Though no one was brave enough to come forward, rumors that soon turned to local superstition swirled around the club and caused a major decline in business. It eventually had to shut down. I watched the building change hands, from a beach café, to a nightclub, until it became the abandoned eyesore it is now.

Subject was asked if she had any more information pertaining to the deaths of Bruno Casas and Filipe Quiroga.

Yes, I believe Mauricio Avila killed them both. I don't know how he got into my house. But I would not put such a thing past him.

Subject was dismissed.

Her Majesty's Cruel Fate

One day as I was seated in my fine
upholstered chair,
I beckoned for my servants, for a tea-cup to
prepare.
But instead of bringing all the parts for me to
stir,
The drink had been already mixed, or so did
I infer.

But as I raised it to my lips, some speckles I
did spy;
Afloat, a group of seeds was drawn into my
line of sight.
Thinking they were merely grains of

lamiaceae,

I raised the tea cup once again and drank it

anyway.

Suddenly, I noted a quite questionable

taste,

Its normal minty flavors were with bitterness

replaced.

I seized a nearby looking glass for to inspect

my eyes,

And noticed then that both of them had

seemed to shrink in size.

Then, I felt as if a brick was placed upon my

chest,

Forcing me to lift it every time I took a

breath.

My difficulty breathing left me feeling quite

fatigued,

As I fought to keep myself from falling prey

to sleep.

Just before the slumber could implant its
claws in me,
I mustered all the strength I had to rise up
from my seat.
I found a pen and paper with which to
record my tale,
And now that you have read it know this,
justice must prevail.

A Peregrine

Please note: this poem is structured experimentally based on synonym-antonym patterns.

A peregrine, a cardinal sin,

A sainted king, the Sultan's kin.

A rival clan, the family's plan,

A random town, a foreign land.

That bitter Fall, the Autumn ball,

Near Krasniy Square, the box-like wall.

A deep ravine, obscure dark green,

Like words unread, and things unseen.

The Shoelacers

No one is unemployed in Pomeroy, and no one is homeless. But no one ever leaves Pomeroy, and no one retires. Pomeroy himself, James William Pomeroy, lives in a mansion overlooking his namesake town. Everyone else inhabits bunkhouses.

It was first Pomeroy Boot Company. Then it became the distinguished Pomeroy Shoes. Now, it is just Pomeroy, a large factory that mimics a community of sorts. People of all ages are employed there, as it has been for the last eighty years. They all work in the center, they eat in the center, and their bunk houses are on the outskirts.

"You ever wish you coulda picked a different job?" the young man asked the old one.

The old man lowered his coffee mug. "What would I've picked?" His hands shook, yet his voice carried confidence.

"I dunno, like an executive or something. Something where you'd make real money and not just rations."

The old man was called Reginald Shoelacer, but he was Old Reg to most. Among the most was his son, Benjamin "Benji" Shoelacer, who sat across from him at a red-and-white folding card table.

Old Reg chuckled. "You don't pick to be an executive."

"Well, you don't pick to be anything, y'know. Just think, Dad, what do you really want to be?"

His face grew stern as he stared at his coffee. "I'd like to be a Shoelacer, like the three generations of Shoelacers that worked in this factory before you. There's pride in being one; don't you ever forget that."

The Shoelacers lived next door to the Bootstitchers and Solemakers. Their cabins were small, and their families were rather large; but they didn't particularly care for discussing the state of things.

In that way, Old Reg was a stubborn man. Stubborn is what country folk like to call someone who is wont to be an all-around pain to deal with. His wispy gray hair stuck nearly straight up from his head, as if in protest of his grouchy brain. However, it's likely safe to assume that it wasn't all his fault. Just like a baby learns to speak from those that surround them, Old Reg's stubbornness was just a reflection of the system he was planted in.

Not much else was planted around Pomeroy. It hosted a harsh climate and an arid terrain. There the sun showed its favor in a most unfavorable way.

Benji gazed out the cabin window upon miles of sand. His father's voice pulled his wandering mind back to the card table.

"You been thinking about Initiation, son?"

He rested his chin on his knuckles. "Not much to think about."

"It don't change a thing if it's not much to think about. You'd make a way."

"S'pose so." Benji sat awkwardly for a few moments before rising and dusting off his pants.

"Just don't let it trouble you. Ain't nothing's gonna happen that's not been happening for the past hundred years or so." He slurped down the last drop of coffee.

Benji, upon returning to his bunk, donned his beige uniform with his last name embroidered on the front. He ran his fingers along the black stitching. The truth was that he had indeed been thinking about Initiation, especially about how much he dreaded it. Hundreds, maybe thousands of eighteen-year-olds like him had walked that stage and professed their loyalty to the workforce. He didn't feel nervous, unlike the many girls who would cake on their makeup and rehearse their walk in hopes of potentially finding a husband at the event. Those who didn't were practically hopeless. No, he felt nothing like them. Their anxiety brought them shivers and shakes and made the whole room feel drafty or sweltering or something or another. His was green. Green like a headache. Green like the moss that covers a stone who won't roll. Green like yucky old stagnation. He wanted something new, or at least slightly different. Maybe not a revolution, but a sliver of light; a cracked door that might lead him to a future of freedom. However, it's sometimes painful to put in the effort of squeezing through cracked doors when the rest of the world's still on the couch. Things aren't changed by stones who don't roll, but moss looks mighty comfortable, too.

Benji accompanied his family to work as usual that day. He sat next to his great-great uncle, Charlie Shoelacer, as he toiled over his labor. Charlie's hands looked like nothing more than a jumbled mess of veins and bones, covered by a sheer blanket of speckled skin. His fingers had grown frail from decades of lacing shoes. He winced in pain almost every time he pulled a lace taut.

Benji examined the room around him and saw many like Charlie, and he watched as several fought to push a needle through swatches of thick leather. Others, with looks of frustration growing upon their faces, struggled to match the thread to their needle's eye. He turned again to the aging man next to him. After years of meticulous work, would Charlie's weathered hands and weak eyes be his only compensation? When would he ever rest?

Benji's workday passed slowly, and he made his way home as soon as the sun set below the distant plateaus. He picked up every scrap of metal he found along the path. He even gathered discarded items from the bins. They'd all go to waste, anyway. He answered no one who questioned him and stayed up all night despite requests to put out his kerosene lamp. When morning came, it was finished.

The Thing was small, but it worked wonderfully and could be easily tucked out of sight under his bunk. He did not fear discovery. Initiation would commence in only a matter of days, and there he could reveal his masterpiece to all of Pomeroy.

The following days moved like water trickling from a dry tap. When the time had finally come, Benji no longer felt anxiety of any form. He had rehearsed his moment so many times that he felt as if it had already happened.

A visibly shaking blonde girl approached the podium before him. "I, Sally Laceweaver, pledge my loyalty to my family, my craft, my..." She froze and stared at the crowd for an uncomfortable amount of time. "my- um, the village of Pomeroy and to the betterment of the industry." As if thirty others hadn't done the same mundane thing before she had, the crowd erupted with applause, and the dean of the Educational Center awarded her a medal. Benji was ushered to the podium next, as the students were ordered by birthdate and not alphabetically.

"May I please say something first?" he asked. The Dean raised an eyebrow but did not stop him. "I am extremely grateful for the education I've received here in Pomeroy." The Dean smiled proudly, and a few mutters of approval arose from parents. "I've been taught an appreciation for fixing things, and I've learned how to do it. I want to show you something." He produced the Thing from a small bag. "This is the New Shoelacer." The crowd gasped. "Now, wait, just listen. I was working, and I realized-" It was becoming difficult to speak over the room. "Don't you see how hard our old folks work?" He held the machine in the air. "Please, listen. This laces shoes for them so they don't have to wear out their hands. Soon I can make a New Lacestitcher, a New Solemaker, and all sorts of other things!"

The Dean placed a hand on his shoulder. "You'd best step off the stage, son."

Benji watched the faces around him turn from disapproval to rage as two teachers led him out of the room. They sternly instructed him to wait in the Dean's office until Initiation was finished.

"I don't know what you were thinking, but you've disgraced your family and our Education Center," said the Dean upon entering. Benji's mother and father entered shortly after. They sat silently in chairs next to him with solemn looks on their faces. The Dean stared at the window for a very long time. "Benjamin, it is an honor to work. It gives life meaning. You just stood in front of our entire community and threatened to deprive them of meaningful living."

"But sir, they're in pain!" cried Benji.

The Dean sighed. "Have you ever felt that kind of pain? It clouds your mind. You don't know what you want. Here, they are well provided for, and they still have meaning to their lives."

Benji shot up from his chair. "How do you know what's a meaningful life when this is the only one you've ever known?"

"Sit down and be silent! Your machine will be discarded tomorrow. You will not be exempt from severe consequences." He turned to Benji's father. "Reginald, please step into the hall with me."

Old Reg got up slowly from his seat. He

looked upon Benji with immeasurable disappointment written on his face. "Why'd you go put our family name on that disgraceful machine?" he muttered, almost incomprehensibly. He left the room without another word after glancing again at his family.

The door closed with a screaming creak and a loud bang. Benji and his mother lingered in heavy silence. Finally, her whispery voice pierced the air with a sigh. "You know, that wasn't a very Christian thing of you to make. You looked like a zealot."Benji lifted his face, but did not look at her. "Sometimes I just wonder if God deals more kindly with zealots than with people who do nothing and accept the ugly state of things."

The Devil Drives a Black Volga

The streets are bare in Krasnodar,

Where children used to play;

In every home in Altai Krai,

They hide themselves away.

A mother whispers at Grandmother's door,

About young Anya's claims;

A classmate has gone missing,

And the Devil is to blame.

A car was seen on the south side of town,

Far too lavish for its locale;

Suspicious, children wish to look,

And soon, indeed they shall.

Mothers worry all through the night,
As policemen are making their rounds;
Fathers whisper behind closed doors,
"They're running us into the ground."

Children talk, so they must not know,
Who is lurking in the streets;
There's less risk in blaming the Evil One,
Lest the children are wont to repeat.

Listen to the winds of change,
For Time is their lawgiver;
But the Devil drives a black Volga,
And he steers a mighty river.

He lies in wait in quiet waters,
Where fishermen dare not glean;
Beneath its depths, the river black
Holds evil myst'ries unseen.

Serpents, vodyanoy[3], and fearsome beings
Crawl along the sandy floor;
And all who wish to wander near,
Soon will be no more.

Listen to how the river flows,
For Time is its lawgiver;
But the Devil drives a black Volga,
And he steers a mighty river.

---

[3] Ichthyic or amphibious Eastern European
river demons.

The Philosophy of Blue Jeans

I find it interesting that nobody notices blue jeans. You could likely match an Hermès belt with an inexpensive pair of jeans and the average eye wouldn't catch on. And maybe that's for the best, because most folks don't need to be spending a fortune on plain old pants after purchasing a five-hundred-dollar belt.

I lived in Paris back then. The war was over, but whispers of espionage still lingered in the air. The neighborhood gossips kept busy with the notions that the plane flying overhead may be a bomber, or perhaps the grocer was a German spy.

Nevertheless, Parisians remained Parisians. My neighbor who could barely afford rent still wore Chanel to work each day. Some women, ironically, even wore plastic bags over their feet to shield their Louboutins from the ashy, war-scarred sidewalks. The fashion world was unified about moving on from the war as quickly as possible, but we were divided on a simple matter: blue jeans.

"Women of class ought not to wear workers' pants and so degrade their elegance!" shouted one side of the debate. The opposing side, infatuated with the newly released American Western films, thought blue jeans were quite alright. I believe Paris has always been somewhat progressive, and this is why denim was all the rage despite the contempt of conservative mothers.

I wasn't particularly rich in those days. As a matter of fact, I owned only one pair of jeans and two or three blouses. I lived in stark contrast to the woman who rode past my apartment each day, her wealth and extravagance displayed in her famed monochrome outfits. Madame Albescu was a successful designer and Romanian countess, and there was no one on Earth whom I hated more. When all of France was dressing in cheap cotton due to war rations, she rode into town in taffeta and organza. When every designer halted their collections to conserve materials, Chateau d'Albescu only raised their prices. What's more, all attempts to escape her were futile. The old witch was my boss.

Everyone at work despised her. She was controlling, demanding, unreasonable, and simply harsh. She was an older woman, and the only joy we found in that wretched workplace were jokes about the inevitability of her demise. In fact, we had a little saying with which we would wish each other farewell: "Que la sorcière attrape un rhume!" or, "May the witch catch a cold!" Perhaps we meant it, and perhaps we did not. Be that as it may, not a soul anticipated the silence of the streets on that Monday morning. The distinctive sound of Madame Albescu's Cadillac was not to be heard, and the crowd that typically gathered to watch her stood confused like children who were cheated out of their Christmas presents.

She was found dead in her home with a glass of poisoned wine spilled beside her. Several rolls of her signature taffeta were reported missing, along with a pair of blue jeans. She never once wore them, so nobody really cared about the blue jeans.

I was invited to her funeral, although I did not wish to be. As a matter of fact, I was invited to give a speech. She had hundreds of fans and followers, but no one was close to her. Only her workers knew her well-crafted image enough to give a proper eulogy.

I wore my brand-new blue jeans to work the next day. A part of me worried that they would be noticeable, but nobody notices blue jeans.

The Debt to the Sea

Part I

A score and sixteen years ago,

When just a child was I,

The ocean's voice did beckon me,

Its beauty caught my eye.

Gazing from my window,

To the vast and deep green sea,

I longed to leave my fortress

To answer its sweet plea.

I quitted my guarded chambers,

Closed quietly my door,

And escaped to find the haven

The Devil Drives A Black Volga

Where the tides doth ebb the shore.

I could not stay on the sand for long,
For the waters called to me,
In the form of whispered angel songs
Like voices soft and sweet.

But as I stepped from the water's edge,
The sky broke loose with flames,
I endeavored to swim back to the shore
But I failed to escape Orcus's aim.

The waves arose, and the Tempest grew
fierce,
As the sea-daemons grasped at my soul;
The creatures and ocean were bent to his
will
By the trident of Neptune he stole.

No longer could I keep my head from the
waves,
My life began to slip from my reach,

But the storm did subside, and I opened my
eyes
To find myself back on the beach.

And though I was safe, my price was not
paid,
Ransomed was I, but not free;
I owed a new favor I could not repay
For a favor had been done for me,
A favor I never could flee:
An unpayable debt to the sea.

Part II
Time carried on, as time does best,
But each year merely felt like a day;
For by anxiously waiting for something to
come,
One will wish all their time away.

My kinsmen arranged a meeting for me,
In hopes of relieving my dread;
She was an acquaintance of mine by the

name of Noelle,

And in a month's time we were wed.

We boarded a ship and set sail for France,

But our journey brought only despair,

For while on the boat, we were met by the

Sea

And the creatures that resided there.

As merely a whisper, the voices began;

But then into a murmur they grew,

Until the buzz of a thousand wails and cries

Emerged from the ocean blue.

I hid from them as best I could,

But they attended me without cease;

Steadfastly stalking me as their prey,

They allowed me no rest or peace.

But on that misty midnight, they reached

from the deep,

The creatures discovered my bride,

From their sepulchres, the daemons arose
To pluck sweet Noelle from my side.

Though with ardour, I ran to chase after her
captors,
No man can ensnare such a ghost,
For before I could fully behold the beings,
Her soul left its humanly host.

Into the water, her silhouette sank,
While I leaned, weeping, over the bow;
The captain, sailors, and boatmen
approached me,
And led me to where I stand now.
 So, now that you've gathered my story,
O Judge, I implore you to liberate me,
For these men believe that she died at my
hands,
But I never could do such a thing.

When Sadness
Seals My Lips

A raven spies my silent cries,

Where the sun has fully dipped;

I long to sing my sorrow here,

But sadness seals my lips.

I ponder great and fearful things,

Here amongst the flower beds;

I contemplate and conjure words,

But they stay within my head.

If only I could utter but a faint and stifled
sound,

Instead, I lie in silence still, for fear I might be

found.

Only birds would listen here; only garden
sprites;

Yet I wonder what they'd whisper if they
saw me where I hide.

Alas, I wait in darkness,

With this bitter cup I sip;

Tomorrow I may speak again,

Though sadness seals my lips.

On the Road to Llanfair

or, Letters to the House of Aylmer in Gloucestershire

Letter I

From Scotland I have travelled,

To seek out a new land;

For Campbell's lords have sieged and placed

My estate in their command.

The Scots will not defend me,

Not Chisholm, not MacEntyre;

Henceforth, I journeyed to the South,

To hide in Gloucestershire.

But at your castle's entrance,
I was turned away by guards;
And forced to travel further still,
Though I had traveled far.

Now to Llanfair I set out,
Through the Cornish Bodmin Moor;
And unless I find new land to claim,
I must journey forevermore.

Letter II
Dear Aylmer, you must listen
To what wondrous things I've seen;
For now I know all secrets
Of what was and soon will be.

Two nights ago, I witnessed
A brilliant crystal lake;
The waters danced to songs that told
The myst'ries of my fate.

143

Alas, I saw the Lady,

Though lady she was not;

But Faerie of the Loch,

Near

Llanfairpwllgwyngyllgogerychwyrndrobwlllla

ntysiliogogogoch[4].

With silver sword and shield in hand,

She crossed the gleaming sea;

She lifted up her radiant face,

To prophesy to me:

"Son of Duncan," the Faerie spoke,

"You have lived to pass through the Moor,

You have proved to be the worthy one

To unlock Llanfair's Door.

"Where life and death are obsolete,

---

[4] Welsh. Pronounced, "lan-fire-pwill-gwin-gyh-go-ger-ikh-wirn-drob-will-lan-tee-sil-ee-oh-go-go-gokh".

Beyond this ancient door;
Eternal things are made complete,
To reign forevermore."

And so, dear Aylmer, I conclude
These letters with a plea:
When all your ships are lost at sea,
When your lords are kept by lock and key,
When your land forfeits its luxuries,
Do not cry out to me.

For here I have resigned to stay,
Though worthy I am not;
To rule Criostail Loch[5],
In
Llanfairpwllgwyngyllgogerychwyrndrobwlllla
ntysiliogogogoch.

---

[5] Scots Gaelic. "Crystal Lake".

老 壮 士 在 哪 里 ？

老壮士在哪里？

静止在山脉吗？

我在问我自己，

我们杀不杀了他？

Lǎo Zhuàngshì Zài Nǎlǐ?

Lǎo zhuàngshì zài nǎlǐ?

Jìngzhǐ zài shānmài ma?

Wǒ zài wèn wǒ zìjǐ,

Wǒmen shā bù shāle tā?

Where is the Old Warrior?

Where is the old warrior?

Is he lying still in the mountains?

I ask myself,

Did we kill him?

A Gardener's Lament

There lived a little flower,

On my dusty window-sill;

Clothed in robes of yellow—

Twas my little daffodil.

How safe I kept my daffodil,

But flowers cannot stay;

For Nature is a greedy soul,

Who steals all things away.

I argued much with Nature,

For my little plant to keep;

But her always-sharpened sickle

Had come prepared to reap.

And though I fought and battled,
My flower was ensnared;
And now my lonely window-sill
Forever remains bare.

The Thieves

Beyond the hills proceed the thieves,
Through deserts vast and bare;
Advancing towards an ancient road,
To seek out treasure there.

And there indeed does treasure lie,
Where I, too, do advance;
Traveling with spice and gold,
Across the wide expanse.

The Identity of Time

Time, as we know it, is a peculiar concept. For it is not a concept merely known by humanity, but one built and birthed of humanity. Though it is a construct, the invention of Earth's wisest populace, it is somehow an inescapable invention (as it has proven thus far impossible to exist apart from it). The fact that one cannot escape time or proceed back and forth through it as a peripatetic unveils a new face of time's mysterious persona: its solidity. Therefore, attributing place-like qualities to it or thinking of it as a traversable state of one's existence is arguably fallacious.

However, fallacy is seldom avoided within the activity of daily life. One would not waste a moment pondering the identity of time when they are on the cusp of lateness to an important meeting. One would never think to equate the clack of their heeled footwear against the pavement to the continuous ticking of a clock, using each step to count a second. Perhaps if she had done this, Margaret would have arrived on time.

She was a woman prone to tardiness, but not of her own volition. She was certainly not lazy, and she often paid careful attention to arise at an appropriate hour each morning. The amount of time allotted to her was simply never enough. Despite her mortification at the thought of being late yet again, she scaled her steel tower-like workplace by way of elevator until she reached her floor. It was a short ride, for those on the lower rungs of the corporate ladder were employed accordingly on the lower floors.

Margaret spent nearly the entirety of the meeting in the back of the room with a downward-facing visage. Another worker had been caught gambling with their time over the company's phone. Human Resources was called in, and all employees were lectured on the rules and practicalities they were far too familiar with. *Your time is precious. Your time from 9:00 to 5:00 is the company's property. Participating in personal activities during these hours is a punishable offense. Gambling with time is a federal offense.*

She no longer feared lateness to these mundane briefings, but she was horrified of lateness in regards to something greater. The briefings, the meetings, the seminars; none of these inspired such motivation in her to hurry out of bed, skip steps in her morning routine, or risk a twisted ankle on the sidewalk. Far more important was the appointment she would plan to pursue subsequent to her meeting. After it dispersed (the meeting, that is), she rushed out of the conference room, not greeting nor farewelling a single soul.

She took the elevator again, this time without stopping until she reached the top floor. At last, an intimidating pair of mahogany doors stood before her. She halted abruptly for a moment before proceeding to push the doors open just enough to allow her entry. The receptionist, the guardian of the illustrious office of the top floor, was absent. After glancing around the room she previously thought she would never live to see, Margaret approached the closed doors of the office chamber in front of her.

Much to her surprise, the doors were not nearly as heavy as they appeared. A desk stood near the back wall. A person could barely be seen sitting in the tall, backwards-turned chair, but only their golden locks peeking out from the side of the chair made it evident they were there at all. Quietly and meekly, Margaret voiced her presence upon entering.

"Could I have a moment of your time?"

If voices could possess color, the regal, feminine voice that responded would certainly be gold. Its keeper made no attempt to turn around or face her, but retorted quickly with a flourish of her neatly manicured hand.

"Could you afford it?"

Margaret fell silent. Too ashamed to leave or proceed with the conversation, she took to awkwardly observing the room around her. The blonde-haired woman continued to speak as she did so.

"Time is a commodity, you know. Each second possesses value." The woman paused momentarily. "Perhaps a sort of stock market should be created for time. I would certainly invest in it." She paused again, but this time only to briefly bask in her extensive understanding before establishing the final point of her monologue. "The value of time spent with a person increases with the intrinsic social value of the person, correct?"

Margaret muttered an affirmative to signify that she had both heard and comprehended her addresser's words. The gesture was accepted, but it was a bluff.

The woman turned around in her chair, finally allowing her face to be seen. "Why are you here, Margaret?"

As soon as the words had left her mouth, the receptionist rushed into the room with an expression of worry and regret. "Madame Bonavich, my sincerest apologies—"

Ms. Bonavich cut her off instantly with a

wave of her hand. "Give us one more moment, please." Her assistant nodded understandingly and backed out of the office. The executive's attention returned to Margaret. "As I was saying, do you know why you are here?"

Quite suddenly, Margaret became aware of a certain fogginess preventing her from recalling the purpose of the meeting. She searched the room for an answer, but her eyes fell back to Ms. Bonavich upon failing to produce one.

The corporate monarch looked on her with compassion, an act unusual of her kind. "Go home, Margaret. Your clock resets soon. You can't afford to stay."

Her eyes lingered on the woman for just a moment before she turned away. As she pushed open the double doors that ushered her back to her life of monotony, she realized her stance of juxtaposition. The doors were like a mirror, but one that reflects only contrast rather than similarity. She looked back once more, then stepped through the wooden gates.

She pondered the day's events on her journey home. The feeling of a stranger calling to you by name is remarkably eerie, but the feeling diminishes if the stranger is passing you on the street. You are likely to soon find that the call was directed towards your fellow name-bearer who happened to be next to you. However, the feeling only intensifies when you are alone in a room with the head of your company. *Go home, Margaret,* she had said. *You can't afford to stay.*

***

The doors were slowly cracked open and the bashful receptionist slipped inside.

"Madame?"

"Yes?"

She descended into the lavish seating accommodation across from the desk.

"Why do you let her come in here every day?"

"I believe she's trapped." Ms. Bonavich responded. "They all are. They all have a certain amount of time allotted to them each day, and they all spend it striving after the same thing. Except, Margaret is different. Everyone spends their days trying to climb the ladder, but Margaret is the only one who gets to the top. However, by the time she gets here, the clock strikes five, she runs out of time, and her mind is cleared. She no longer can remember her purpose for being here until her clock resets again the following morning.

"I believe I have explained my concept of time as a commodity before, yes?" The receptionist nodded. "Excellent. Think of it this way. I have purchased eight hours of my workers' days, nine o' clock to five o' clock. Their time is mine to do with as I please; it is my slave. But to them, even their own time is their master. Their clock makes every decision for them. So, to answer your question, I give Margaret my time because I enjoy it. The eternal race of the proletariat is one that quite truly fascinates me. I think that there is likely a sliver of my conscience in which I would like to see the clock pushed back an hour so that just once, Margaret can make it on time."

The receptionist leaned forward ever so slightly. "But might you feel ashamed of this system?"

"Why should I be? It took me years to get here, to buy more time—but it only takes her a day. Everyone wants to be where I am, but the little morsels of freedom I place in front of them distract them from ever getting there. I give them one day a week to dress casually to distract them from the monotony of their uniforms. I give them salaries so that they learn to sell me their time. These things are meaningless. I had to vanquish the desire of these freedoms, but Margaret is naturally immune. If one day she is able to overcome her battle with her clock, then so be it. But even this is meaningless, because we all in due course will run out of time."

There's a Dead
Man in the Parlor

There's a dead man in the parlor,

Spilling tea upon the floor.

He was once my close companion,

But he isn't anymore.

He was whispering with Birdie,

About her fancy brand-new shoes;

And I knew she didn't buy them,

But I think he knew so, too.

He was always close to Birdie,

But even closer recently;

He's been sneaking to her parlor,

For what he claims is merely tea.

Now he's slouched upon the floorboards,

Because he was a cheating man;

There's a dead man in the parlor,

And the gun is in my hands.

The Looking Glass

Dearest reader, please note that I have intentionally omitted nearly all punctuation that would be indicative of dialogue. I aim to present a very subtle shift between narrative and dialogue in the name of artistic experimentation, and also to perhaps incite a little bit of confusion. Enjoy.

When asked to describe my friends, I say there are none or few. I do not know which is correct. I am a woman of hyperbole. I find solace in exaggerating myself in the lives of my acquaintances. Where there is brief

recognition, a passing glance, or subtle moments of bavardage, I interpret it as the inception of a blossoming friendship.
Should I know my place instead? I do. I am not fond of it.
I like to think that Mr. Li upstairs and Collins downstairs are at least aware of me; their admiration is unnecessary to me but I do grasp at acknowledgement.
It was Collins who met me on the stairs yesterday. He told me I bear a resemblance to my sister. I told him I agree, but how does he know my sister?
He told me he was the one who found her. Yes, if her eyes beneath the shining waters were not brown unlike mine, he would have thought she was walking today. Besides, her name and face were in the papers.
I wished not to speak of my sister, but I wished to end the conversation even less.
She could have been a Gibson Girl, he said. If only she had become famous.
I knew this.
She used to pose for paintings when that was a popular thing to do. She had the kind of hair that shone without pomade, which is the kind of woman that is chosen for pomade advertisements.
I found myself to be very plain next to her. But I choose to put that out of my mind these days.
We stood outside my door. My weariness of the topic at hand was beginning to

overwhelm my eagerness to converse. I put my hand on the door.

He asked, may he come in?

I said of course, sir.

I found the sofa and reclined, but not fully. I told him to come and sit if he'd like. He did exactly so. He was then very silent for a period of time.

That is a very fine looking glass, he told me. I thanked him. It was my mother's.

It was silent again.

Tell me, I asked, how did you find her?

He asked if, by that, do I inquire of how he came across her, or in what state was she when she was found?

I asked for both, please.

He found her on his morning walk. He saw something of particularly strange texture floating in the shallow creek, and soon discovered it to be human hair. It was attached to a human body, a deceased one. And as for her condition, her eyes were shut and she was very pale. There were three small punctures in her neck. A very peculiar sight indeed.

He then asked me if I miss her.

Yes, of course, what an inappropriate question!

I found him staring at the looking glass again for an uncomfortable amount of time. Was there a problem with it?

He said no, but it is noticeably crooked. Is there a reason why?

Certainly not, said I, as I arose to adjust it. It seemed straight enough.

No, no, not in that way. He tilted his head. It just appears to protrude from where it hangs.

How odd. It must be an issue with the wall. I told him I would take it up with the landlady. He insisted he would help and got up despite my protests.

He fiddled with it and even shook it a little bit before feeling something unusual in the back. Why, there's an object taped to the back of this thing! He paused for a moment. Tell me, please, he said, what's behind this looking glass?

I feigned surprise. I haven't the slightest idea!

He stepped closer to me and promised I could tell him.

I knew it all along that I could trust him; that he was the only one who understood me or appreciated me. Though he had never spoken with me before, I always knew we were friends.

Oh, Mr. Collins, I cried, you have no idea how I have been dying to tell somebody! You must understand how difficult of a sister she was, what, with her beauty and congeniality and all—she had so many friends, and I had none! I never thought of hurting her, not once, not until it was late at night and I was having one of my usual fits of loneliness and perhaps a little bit of jealousy. She was staying the night in this apartment right here, so I snuck over to where she slept and-

I told him to examine the back of the looking glass. He produced a large fork.

Yes, that's it! Yes, I crept over to where she was laying and I poked her in the neck with it! I cleaned it up nicely, don't you think so? But please, I said to him, you must understand I am not the killing kind! That's why I set her in that creek; I wanted her to be in a peaceful place. I truly am merciful, Mr. Collins, I do swear.

He said he believed me. He thanked me for telling him.

But that was when he brought out that disgraceful badge.

He had been a police officer this whole time and I didn't know it. That's why they assigned him to this case- he was the closest individual to me and yet I knew nothing about him.

Isn't it horrid? Isn't it all horrid?

I would like to think that none of this would have happened if he hadn't looked behind the looking glass. But a looking glass is a looking glass, after all, and all it can do is reflect the truth.

About the Author

J. Elmore is a writer of poetry and short fiction from Atlanta, Georgia. Some of her earliest inspirations come from Edgar Allan Poe and Emily Dickinson, and she has recently been influenced by the works of Jack Kerouac, Izumi Shikibu, Ono no Komachi, and Neil Gaiman. She is extremely passionate about words and the city where she lives. Her favorite hobby outside of writing is studying languages, and she speaks English, Russian, Mandarin, Spanish, Portuguese, and Korean with varying levels of proficiency.

She invites you to visit her website- www.jelmorebooks.com, and find her on Instagram and TikTok.

Acknowledgments

All Russian entries were written with the help of Titus and Anya Hanham.

All Mandarin entries were written with the help of Caitlin Khan and Shine Lee.

"Sonhadora" é dedicada a Yasmin, Jennifer, Júlia, e todas as minhas amigas queridas no Brasil.

Made in United States
Orlando, FL
31 July 2023